The
MAYA

Revised and Updated

JANE SHUTER

Heinemann Library
Chicago, Illinois

©2002, 2009 Heinemann Library
a division of Pearson Inc.
Chicago, Illinois

Customer Service 888-454-2279
Visit our website at www.heinemannraintree.com

Photo research by Mica Brancic
Designed by Richard Parker and Manhattan Design
Printed and bound in China by CTPS

13 12 11 10 09
10 9 8 7 6 5 4 3 2 1

New edition ISBNs: 978-1-4329-1330-4 (hardcover)
                       978-1-4329-1338-0 (paperback)

The Library of Congress has cataloged the first edition as follows:
Shuter, Jane
The Maya / Jane Shuter
p. cm. – (History opens windows)
Includes bibliographic references and index.
Summary: Presents an overview of Mayan culture, discussing their government, religion, domestic life, recreation, occupations, entertainment, food, shelter, and clothing.
ISBN 978-1-58810-591-2 (1-58810-591-1) (HC) ISBN 978-1-4034-0026-0 (1-4034-0026-1) (PBK)
Mayas – History – Juvenile Literature. 2. Mayas – Social Life and customs – Juvenile Literature. [1. Mayas. 2. Indians of Central America.] 1. Title. II. Series.
F1435 .S546 2002
972. 81'01 – dc21

2001004028

Acknowledgments
The author and publishers are grateful to the following for permission to reproduce photographs: p. 6 © Kimbell Art Museum/Corbis; pp. 7, 18, 21, 23, 25 © Justin Kerr; p. 8 © Werner Forman/Art Resource; p. 10 © Michael Freeman/Corbis; p. 11 © Charles and Josette Lenars/Corbis; pp. 12, 13 © Gianni Dagli Orti/Corbis; pp. 14, 20, 28 © D. Donne Bryant/Art Resource; p. 16 © Eric Lessing/Art Resource; pp. 19, 30 © SEF/Art Resource; p. 22 © Michel Zabe/Art Resource; p. 24 © Dr. Kurt Stavenhagen Collection, Mexico City/Werner Forman/Art Resource; p. 26 © Getty Images/The Image Bank/Macduff Everton; p. 29 © Scala/Art Resource.

Illustrations: p. 4 Eileen Mueller Neill; pp. 9, 15, 17, 27 Juvenal "Marty" Martinez.
Cover photograph reproduced with permission of © Lonely Planet Images/Richard l'Anson.

Contents

Some words are shown in bold, **like this**.
You can find out what they mean by looking in the glossary.

Introduction

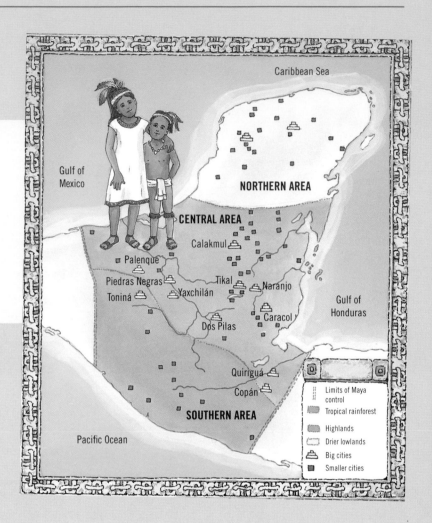

This map shows the areas where the Maya lived and ruled.

Caribbean Sea

Gulf of Mexico

NORTHERN AREA

CENTRAL AREA

Calakmul

Palenque

Piedras Negras

Tikal

Yaxchilán

Naranjo

Toniná

Gulf of Honduras

Dos Pilas

Caracol

Quiriguá

Copán

SOUTHERN AREA

Pacific Ocean

Limits of Maya control
Tropical rainforest
Highlands
Drier lowlands
Big cities
Smaller cities

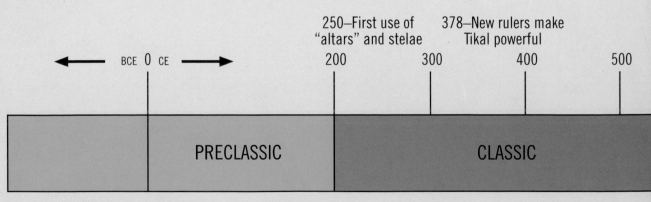

250—First use of "altars" and stelae

378—New rulers make Tikal powerful

BCE 0 CE

200   300   400   500

PRECLASSIC	CLASSIC

Mayans living in villages. Larger villages have a temple in the center.

200—First stone temples and ballcourts at Copán

250— Glyphs in use

426—New rulers make Copán powerful

The Maya people became powerful in Central America from about 250 CE to 900 CE. Today the land they controlled covers Guatemala, Belize, and parts of Mexico, El Salvador, and western Honduras.

The land and weather of the area made farming and building difficult. There were mountains in the south and rainforests in the center. Even so the Maya farmed the land. They built cities with huge stone palaces and **temples**.

The Maya lived in different **city-states**. We see the Maya as a single group, even though different kings ruled each city-state. All Maya people shared a religion, organized themselves in the same way, and used the same written language. They also used the same calendar system and a similar building style.

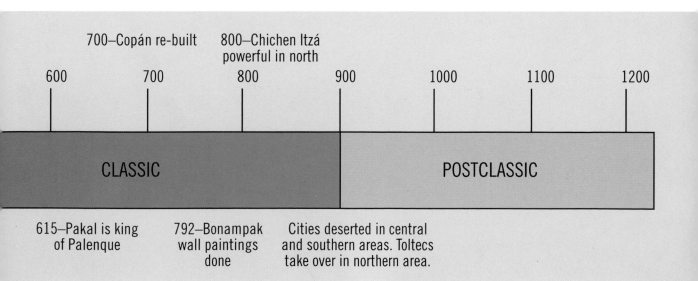

700—Copán re-built   800—Chichen Itzá powerful in north

600	700	800	900	1000	1100	1200

CLASSIC   POSTCLASSIC

615—Pakal is king of Palenque   792—Bonampak wall paintings done   Cities deserted in central and southern areas. Toltecs take over in northern area.

How Were the Maya Ruled?

This clay statue shows a Mayan *ajaw*, dressed for a religious ceremony.

The Maya did not have a single ruler. Each city and the lands around it were ruled by a different **ajaw** (pronounced ah-HAW). An *ajaw* spoke to the gods for his people. He took part in many **ceremonies** wearing masks to show different gods.

Each *ajaw* was seen as chosen by the gods. Sometimes sons ruled after their fathers, so historians think the Maya believed the gods chose a family to rule, not just one person.

An *ajaw* ruled with the help of **nobles**, priests, and **officials**. He lived with his family and servants in a palace in the city. Women rarely ruled, although some queens ruled for their sons until they grew up.

Almost all ordinary people lived in villages and farmed the land. They only went to the cities for religious ceremonies and other **festivals**.

Most Mayan rulers were men. There were only a few women rulers. But the wives of the *ajaws* were important and took part in religious ceremonies. Here the wife of a king is shown having a vision of a serpent ancestor.

City-States

This stone carving shows a captured noble kneeling in front of the *ajaw* "Bird Jaguar," whose army has beaten him. The prisoner is biting his fingers as a sign that he is giving in.

Historians call a Maya city and the land it controlled a **city-state**. Some city-states were more powerful than others. Different city-states were powerful at different times. Sometimes people in different city-states fought one another. Sometimes they traded with each other. A small city-state would often need the help of a larger city-state to protect it. Its **ajaw** would have to obey the *ajaw* of the bigger city.

The *ajaw*, his family, and a large group of **nobles**, priests, and **officials** lived in each city. Their servants also lived in the cities. But most ordinary people lived in nearby villages. Villagers made and grew almost everything they needed. They had to grow enough food to feed the people in the cities, too. This was part of their duty to the *ajaw*.

This modern artist's recreation shows part of the city of Copán, looking from the central square to the **temple** area. All the buildings in this area are temples except for the ball court.

Ball court

Building a City

Temples led to the sky, the home of the gods. They were designed to look as tall as possible.

All buildings in the cities were made from local stone. Most Maya cities had sources of limestone nearby. In the city of Copán, the builders used a volcanic stone. This means that it was made from lava. The stone was soft when it was dug out, but it hardened over time. Every city had a Great **Plaza**, where the most important **temples** and the royal palace were built. The rest of the city spread out from the plaza. Big cities had several smaller plazas with temples and other public buildings in them.

Temples and palaces had the same steep shape as the **thatched** roofs of ordinary homes. To get this shape, the builders made a series of steps. Each layer of stones was smaller than the layer below. This is called corbelling. The steps were then filled in or covered over, making a smooth, sloping surface.

Most palaces and temples were probably decorated on the inside. The brightly colored pictures of people, animals, and gods each told a story.

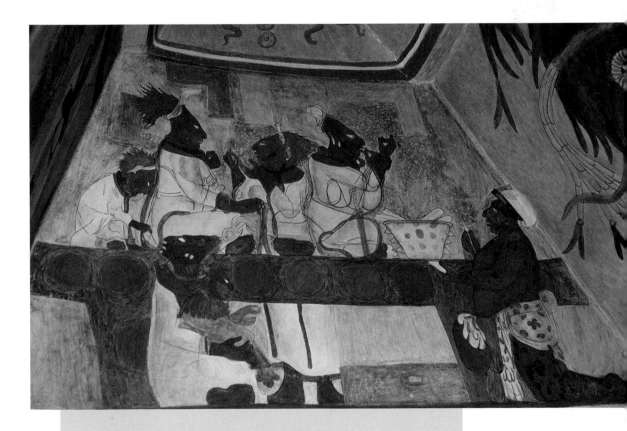

In this decorated room at Bonampak, you can see the shape of the corbelled roof. It has been covered with slabs to make a smooth line.

Religion

The Maya believed in many gods and goddesses. They controlled every part of life, from how the crops grew, to a person's health, to which **city-state** won a war. The Maya kept the gods happy by praying and performing dances, music, and plays. They also gave gifts to the gods, including food and often blood. The Maya religion taught that without gifts of blood, the gods would stop the sun, the rain, and everything else. So a king or priest would give some of his blood in a bowl. But the Maya believed that the gods sometimes wanted a whole life. This could be the life of an animal or even a human.

"Altar stones" like this one were placed in front of many **temples**. We think that the Maya put offerings to the gods on them. *Ajaws* may have stood on them during religious **ceremonies**.

The Maya also believed that the **spirits** of dead relatives could affect their daily lives. These spirits needed gifts, too. They could help you if you were in trouble, but if you did not keep them happy they could cause trouble. Most ordinary people had a **shrine** in their homes. This was a special place where they could pray to their dead relatives.

This pottery oil burner was used in religious ceremonies. It shows an old god sitting on a stool and was found buried with a **noble** in Tikal.

Ball Courts

The ball court at Copán was built right next to a temple. This shows how the game was sometimes linked to religious festivals.

In villages and cities the Maya played a ball game with two teams and a hard rubber ball on a long, thin court. In the villages ball courts were a straight, flat piece of land. In the cities the game became linked to Maya religious beliefs. So the Maya built stone ball courts near **temples**. At important **festivals**, Maya kings played the ball game to defeat death, darkness, and famine (lack of food). They were copying an old story in which the Lords of the Underworld were beaten at a ball game.

The rules of the ball game are not clear. They may even have been different depending on the place and the time.

There were two teams. The number of players on a team was not always the same, but there were probably no more than five.

The ball was not allowed to touch the ground.

The ball was kept moving by bouncing it off the side of the ball court.

The object of the game was to get the ball into the open end of the other team's end of the court.

Temples and Burials

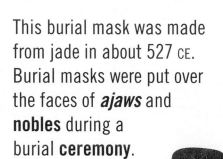

This burial mask was made from jade in about 527 CE. Burial masks were put over the faces of *ajaws* and **nobles** during a burial **ceremony**.

Temples were the homes of the gods. They were the tallest buildings in a Maya city, and the Maya called them "mountains." The **shrine** at the top, the house of the god, was very small and looked like an ordinary Maya house. But because it was a home for a god it was built from stone, which ordinary houses were not. It was also beautifully decorated, inside and out, with carvings and paintings.

Many Maya temples are more than they seem. There are probably several other layers under the temple that you cannot see. Maya kings often rebuilt temples to show how important they thought the gods were. Temples also often hide a king's tomb. Kings were buried under tombs with the things they would need after death, such as clothes and food. Ordinary people were buried under their homes.

The tomb of a Maya *ajaw* named Pakal lies deep under a temple in Palenque.

War

Many Maya carvings show an *ajaw* having his defeated enemies brought to him after he has won a war. It showed his strength and importance. This carving shows captives being brought before a Maya *ajaw*.

An *ajaw* had to prove that he was a good fighter and war leader. This was because Maya **city-states** often fought one another. City-states did not have a full-time army. Instead **nobles** did the fighting. The Maya tried to capture their enemies instead of killing them. Enemy kings were often forced to play the ball game at religious **festivals**. The *ajaw* would make sure that the captured king lost.

The Maya went to war to the sound of trumpets and drums. They fought hand-to-hand, not in organized groups. Their weapons were clubs and stone-tipped spears. They also used daggers with stone blades. For defense, warriors carried small hand-held shields and armor made from many layers of **quilted** cotton cloth.

A warrior could surrender during a battle if he knelt down and held another warrior's leg. Being captured was not a good thing for a noble warrior. They were killed as sacrifices. Ordinary soldiers usually became slaves.

This wall painting is of a battle scene from Bonampak. It shows a tangle of bodies, giving an idea of how confusing hand-to-hand fighting could be. The warrior at the top has a quilted shield.

Food and Farming

The Maya farmed the land around their villages. They used digging sticks to turn the soil. They planted two crops a year. In some areas, farmers grew food on **terraces**. This kept the soil from washing away in heavy rains or floods. In other places they built ponds to trap water for **irrigating** the fields. But they mostly used the slash-and-burn method. This involves cutting down the trees and plants in a field and burning them. Then they planted crops in the ash mixed with soil and let the rain water them.

It was hard to clear the lowland jungle and make the land suitable for farming.

Maya farmers grew corn, beans, and squash in the fields. They also grew avocados, cocoa beans, and fruit trees. There were gardens in the villages where people grew tomatoes, chillis, and peppers. The Maya hunted animals, such as rabbits and deer, for meat. They also fished in rivers or in the sea. The Maya cooked their food over an open fire. They either roasted it or stewed it in a pot in the flames. Ordinary people mainly ate corn porridge, flat bread made with corn flour, and vegetables.

Even ordinary villagers had big collections of plates, pots, and cups. This plate shows a woman grinding corn.

Trade and Work

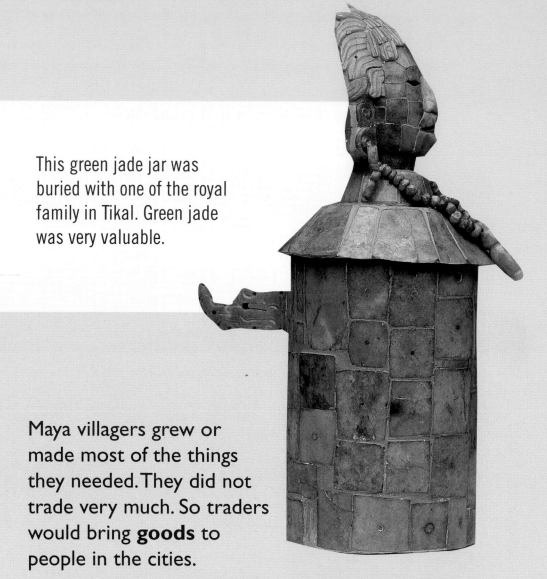

This green jade jar was buried with one of the royal family in Tikal. Green jade was very valuable.

Maya villagers grew or made most of the things they needed. They did not trade very much. So traders would bring **goods** to people in the cities.

Skilled craft workers lived in cities. They used raw materials such as feathers, shells, and precious stones brought in by traders. The craft workers made things for the *ajaws*, **nobles**, and priests. Traders also brought pottery and jewelry to the cities.

Craft workers in different cities had different styles. Other peoples taken over by the Maya had their own styles of pottery and weaving. One of the ways to find out where traders from a **city-state** traveled is to see where their local style of pottery is found. Craft workers sometimes mixed styles of pots or jewelry. For example, they could use a Maya shape for a pot but decorate it in a style used in places their traders visited.

This pot was made by Maya craft workers, but it shows how Maya potters were affected by other styles of pottery. The patterns are Maya, but putting the pot on three legs is a style copied from the people of Teotihuacán.

Families and Clothing

This model shows a Maya woman weaving cloth on a "backstrap" loom. She keeps the long threads tight by tying them to her back and to the branch across her feet.

The Maya lived and worked in large family groups. This was true of villagers as well as royal and **noble** families. Villages were made up of several family groups. This meant that there were enough people to make or grow all the food, cloth, pots, and other **goods** that everyone needed. The men farmed and made pots while the women cooked and wove cloth and baskets. Children learned from their parents and started to work as soon as they were old enough. Only **scribes** went to school.

Most Maya cloth was made from cotton dyed with vegetable dyes. Ordinary workers wore simple clothes that were easy to work in. Men wore **loincloths**, and women wore long skirts and **tunics**. The more important people wore layers of clothing, and the cloth was more brightly colored and decorated. Nobles wore long skirts and tunics or capes. Both men and women wore jewelry and sandals. Some Maya also wore fancy headdresses. The more complicated the headdress, the more powerful the person wearing it was.

This pottery model shows an *ajaw* sitting on his throne. You can tell how important he is because his clothes are so fancy and his ear plugs are so big. They were probably made from jade and would have been very heavy.

Homes

Most Maya lived in villages in one-room rectangular huts. These huts had one door and no windows. The Maya used branches and clay to make the walls. The roof was **thatched** and steep. That way the rain would quickly run off it. The huts had a dirt floor and a hearth (area in front of a fireplace).

In the city, the homes of kings, **nobles**, and priests were made from stone. The rooms were the same shape as a village home, but there were more of them. They were usually plastered and painted in bright colors.

Many of the descendants of the ancient Maya still live in huts with thatched roofs, much like their ancestors.

Most Maya villages were arranged like this one.

Crops were grown around the edges of the village.

Women worked together in the central courtyard.

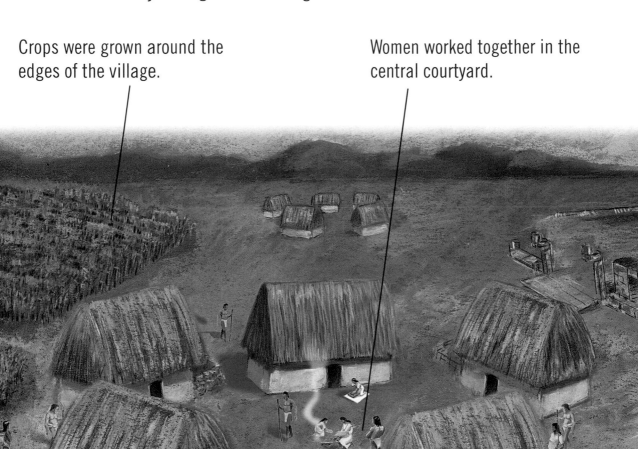

Homes were small, dark, and airless.

The men farmed, while the women ran the homes.

Writing and Calendars

This carving shows the type of pictures used in glyphs. It can be confusing trying to figure out what they mean.

The Maya used a form of picture writing called glyphs. It took a long time to translate them, and even today not everyone agrees about what they mean.

The Maya used glyphs everywhere. They are carved on decorated standing stones called stelae, on altars, and on buildings. They are painted around the edges of plates and cups. They are also painted on long, folding books called codices. The Spanish who invaded in 1519 destroyed all but three of these codices.

The Maya had a very complicated calendar system, with three sets of calendars running at once. There was a "sacred calendar," which had 260 days arranged in 20 months of 13 days. Each day was named after the month and the day. For example, the first day of *Imix*, the first month, was 1 *Imix*. The second day was 2 *Imix*, and so on, up to 13 *Imix*. Then the next month began.

The second calendar was the "vague year." It had 365 days arranged in 18 months of 20 days each, with five extra days at the end of the year. Finally, the Maya had the "long count," which lasted about 400 years. It used differently named and numbered counts of 360 days each.

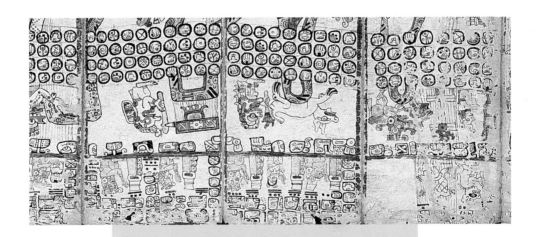

This page from the Madrid Codex has calendar dates running across the middle of the folded page.

End of Empire

The Maya empire did not end suddenly with a takeover by another group. It finished as it began, slowly and over many years. The Maya had abandoned most cities by 900 CE. Why did the Maya leave their cities? No one knows for sure. The population grew, and there was not enough food. Studying skeletons has shown that 90 percent of people were underfed. This may have led the villagers to rise up against their kings, who were supposed to control the crops. Wars between the **city-states** could have gotten out of control. But we may never know what caused the end of the Maya.

People lived in some Maya cities long after 900 CE. But non-Maya people such as the Toltecs ruled them. This carving is in the Toltec style.

Glossary

ajaw Mayan name for their ruler

ceremony set of acts that has religious meaning

city-state city and the nearby towns, villages, and land controlled by the ruler

festival time of celebration

goods things made or grown to trade or swap

irrigate bring water to crops

loincloth material that covers the body between the waist and thighs

noble important person of high birth

official person who runs a country for the ruler

plaza large open square in the center of a city or town

quilted made of several layers of cloth stitched together

scribe person whose job it is to read, write, and keep records

shrine special place for worshipping

spirit being that cannot be seen

temple building where people pray to gods and goddesses

terrace flat land made for farming

thatched having a roof made out of grass or other plants

tunic knee-length belted garment

Find Out More

Books

Eboch, Chris. *Life Among the Maya*. Detroit: Lucent, 2005.

Ganeri, Anita. *Ancient Maya*. Minneapolis: Compass Point, 2006.

Perl, Lila. *The Ancient Maya*. New York: Franklin Watts, 2005.

Websites

www.mayankids.com
Fun facts and games all about the Maya.

www.civilization.ca/civil/maya/mmc04eng.html
This website about the Maya is from the Canadian Museum of Civilization.

Index